P9-AFJ-725

MARTHA

WASHINGTON

FIRST LADY OF THE UNITED STATES

SPECIAL LIVES IN HISTORY THAT BECOME

Signature LIVES

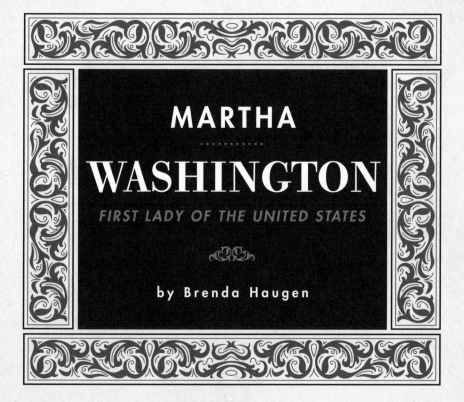

MARTHA

WASHINGTON

FIRST LADY OF THE UNITED STATES

by Brenda Haugen

Content Adviser: Mary V. Thompson,
Research Specialist, Mount Vernon Ladies' Association,
Mount Vernon, Virginia

Reading Adviser: Rosemary G. Palmer, Ph.D.,
Department of Literacy, College of Education,
Boise State University

COMPASS POINT BOOKS ✦ MINNEAPOLIS, MINNESOTA

Compass Point Books
3109 West 50th Street, #115
Minneapolis, MN 55410

Visit Compass Point Books on the Internet at *www.compasspointbooks.com*
or e-mail your request to *custserv@compasspointbooks.com*

Editor: Sue Vander Hook
Lead Designer: Jaime Martens
Page Production: Noumenon Creative
Photo Researcher: Svetlana Zhurkin
Cartographer: XNR Productions, Inc.
Educational Consultant: Diane Smolinski

Managing Editor: Catherine Neitge
Creative Director: Keith Griffin
Editorial Director: Carol Jones

Library of Congress Cataloging-in-Publication Data
Haugen, Brenda
    Martha Washington / by Brenda Haugen
      p. cm. — (Signature Lives)
    Includes bibliographical references and index.

    ISBN 0-7565-0983-1 (hardcover)
    1. Washington, Martha, 1731-1802—Juvenile literature. 2. Presidents'
spouses—United States—Biography—Juvenile literature. I. Title. II.
Series
E312.19.W34H38 2006
973.4'1'092—dc22   2005002707

Signature Lives

REVOLUTIONARY WAR ERA

The American Revolution created heroes—and traitors—who shaped the birth of a new nation: the United States of America. "Taxation without representation" was a serious problem for the American colonies during the mid-1700s. Great Britain imposed harsh taxes and refused to give the colonists a voice in their own government. The colonists rebelled and declared their independence from Britain—the war was on.

Martha Washington

Table of Contents

1 "GOD BLESS LADY WASHINGTON"

Fireworks flashed and boomed when 57-year-old Martha Washington entered the city of Baltimore, Maryland. Musicians played, and journalists hurriedly wrote down all the details of her arrival. Just three weeks before, on April 30, 1789, her husband was inaugurated in New York City as the first president of the United States of America. Now, a huge crowd welcomed the nation's first lady.

From Baltimore, she journeyed on to Philadelphia, Pennsylvania, with her grandchildren Nelly and Washy in tow. There, church bells rang, cannons thundered, and crowds gathered to welcome this beloved woman to the city. Standing up in her horse-drawn carriage, she addressed the enthusiastic crowd. In her naturally gracious way, she

Martha Washington (1731-1802) served as first lady of the United States from 1789 to 1797.

thanked the citizens and the soldiers, who served as her escorts.

Washington stayed in Philadelphia with her friend Molly Morris. But Philadelphia was not her final destination. She was on her way to New York City, the capital of the newly formed United States of America. When it was time to leave Philadelphia, Morris and her two daughters joined the Washingtons. To get to New York, the ladies and their entourage had to cross the Hudson River. There at the river were George Washington and

George Washington arrived in New York City by barge on April 23, 1789, to begin his presidency.

Robert Morris, ready to escort their wives and the children across on a fine barge.

On the other side, a huge crowd gathered to welcome them. The barge landed, cheers broke out, and people chanted, "God bless Lady Washington!" The governor of New York greeted the first lady and escorted her to 3 Cherry St., the house rented by Congress for the president and his wife.

What an important day for this woman the people called their lady! Martha Washington, though, was not dressed in a dazzling gown made of fine imported silk or studded with jewels. Instead, she wore a dress made of homespun material, made in the United States of America.

Three weeks earlier, George Washington had worn an American-made brown suit to his inauguration. It was a silent statement to the American people: The new president and his wife were not a king and queen. They were homespun people—"made in America"—servants of its citizens. After all, the nation had just gained its independence from a king—George III of England—and most people wanted nothing to do with monarchs.

Congress had quite a debate over what to call their new president. Some thought His Serene Highness was appropriate, while others preferred simply President of the United States. One member of Congress wanted to call him "His Highness the

George Washington was inaugurated as president of the United States at Federal Hall in New York City in 1789.

President of the United States of America, and Protector of their Liberties." But Congress chose the simple title, President of the United States, and addressed him as Mr. President. His wife came to be called the first lady.

However, Martha Washington sometimes felt more like a prisoner than a lady. It was decided that the Washingtons should not visit personally with their friends. They should only entertain in a formal or public manner, so it would not look like they were playing favorites. Their house on Cherry Street often was filled with people, but Martha felt confined and separated from her friends. She told her friend Betsey Hamilton, "They call me First Lady in the land and think I must be extremely happy. They might more properly call me the Chief State Prisoner."

In spite of her loneliness and dislike for public life, Martha Washington brought grace and dignity to her position. Their home was a lively place. On Tuesdays, the president greeted gentlemen guests. Every Friday evening, the house was open to anyone who wanted to visit, as long as they were dressed properly.

Martha planned these events and entertained large crowds in her home. Ordinary people arrived every week in their finest clothes to mingle with the top leaders of the country and the most refined in society. Official government receptions and elegant formal dinners were held on other days of the week. The Washingtons entertained almost continuously. Martha enjoyed the events, but she once complained to her niece that she had not had a half hour to herself since she arrived in New York.

Martha Washington would have rather been home at Mount Vernon, Virginia. But she accepted her new life and enthusiastically served the people of the United States. This was not the first time she had

Martha Washington held weekly Friday evening social engagements at her home in New York City.

lived away from Mount Vernon, nor the first time she had served her country. During the nation's struggle for independence, she spent more than 50 months at her husband's Army camps or nearby in hopes they would be able to see each other. She gave her time, energy, and compassion to encourage her husband and his soldiers during the difficult winter months of the American Revolutionary War (1775-1783).

George Washington had served as general of the nation's Army for eight years, and now he was duty-bound to serve his country as its first president. Martha Washington was duty-bound to her husband. She would willingly serve alongside him during his eight years as president. When she became first lady, she wrote:

> *I little thought, when the war was finished, that any circumstances could possibly have happened which would call the general into public life again. ... Though the General's feelings and my own were perfectly in unison with respect to our predilection [preference] for public life, yet I cannot blame him for having acted according to his duties in obeying the voice of his country. ... With respect to myself, I sometimes think the arrangement is not quite as it ought to have been; that I, who had much rather be at home, should occupy a place with which a great many younger and gayer women would be prodigiously [incredibly] pleased.*

Martha Washington served her country well and set a high standard for the position of the president's wife. Although her husband was the head of the infant United States, it has been said the heart of the nation was its first lady—Martha Washington. ℘

2 Young Martha Dandridge

❧⤳✦⤲❧

Martha Washington probably never dreamed she would one day be the most important woman in the country. When she was born on June 2, 1731, her parents, John and Frances Dandridge, most likely never thought their first child would be famous either. No one would have known what was ahead for this baby girl.

Little Martha grew up on a large plantation along the Pamunkey River in New Kent County, Virginia. A plantation typically had a lot of farmland and a large house for the planter's family. Smaller buildings provided housing for slaves and hired servants who worked in the fields of tobacco, cotton, or corn. The Dandridges' two-story home was named Chestnut Grove. Eight children eventually filled the home that also served as their school.

Girls didn't receive a formal education at that time. But John Dandridge made sure his daughters were taught the basics of reading, writing, mathematics, and religion. The boys in the family had a tutor who taught them in their home. The girls probably learned a lot just by listening to their brothers' lessons. It was more important, though, for girls to learn how to run a household, entertain guests, and take care of a family. Someday, they would need those skills when they had families of their own.

Martha enjoyed learning, and she liked her music and dancing lessons. Riding horses, cooking, and gardening also filled much of her day. She grew a large variety of herbs and learned how to use many of them as medicines. Sewing was one of Martha's special talents, and she learned to make fine clothes and create fancy embroidery at an early age.

Martha's family shopped in nearby Williamsburg, Virginia, a very busy town. The streets were lined with shops where coopers made barrels for flour and saddlers crafted leather saddles for horses. The millinery shop was a favorite place for many women of the time. It was not uncommon for a milliner to advertise the arrival of the latest imports from London, such as jewelry, shoes, and buttons. The Dandridge girls may have been fitted there for beautiful gowns made from the finest British silk and satin. Milliners made and

A mother teaches her daughter at home.

sold dresses, petticoats, gloves, cloaks, and hats—
everything a woman might need for entertaining or for
impressing a prospective husband.

Five-foot- (150 centimeters) tall Martha with her
hazel eyes and dark brown hair did attract a suitor
when she was 18 years old. He was one of the most eligible, rich, single men in Virginia—Daniel Parke
Custis. Although 20 years older than Martha, Custis
was captivated by her and wanted to marry her. At
first, Daniel's father, John Custis, was against the mar-

Daniel Parke Custis (1711-1757) was the first husband of Martha Washington.

riage. He thought the Dandridge family was not high enough on the social ladder and not good enough for his son. But Martha charmed him with her gentle, kind character, and he finally consented. Unfortunately, her soon-to-be father-in-law John Custis died before the wedding date.

On May 15, 1750, Martha Dandridge married Daniel Parke Custis and moved to the 17,500-acre (7,000-hectare) estate he had inherited from his father. The house, which was called White House, was located on the Pamunkey River, not far from where Martha had grown up.

Daniel wanted his wife to have more than just a nice home. He sent to England for beautiful clothes he knew Martha would like. He took her to Williamsburg twice a year to stay in the mansion his father had left him there. They went to fancy balls, visited friends, and enjoyed each other's company.

In 1751, Martha gave birth to their first child— Daniel Parke Custis, named after his father. In 1753, they were blessed with a daughter, Frances Parke

Custis. But tragedy followed the next year, when 3-year-old Daniel died. Martha and Daniel deeply mourned the loss of their son. Martha now feared something might happen to Frances, and she became very protective of her. After all, in the mid-1700s, it was not unusual for children to die from one of the many diseases that often plagued the colonies. Many babies died at birth or even before they were born. Sometimes, the mother also died during childbirth.

On November 27, 1754, not long after little Daniel died, Martha had another son, John Parke Custis. They called him Jacky. Then in 1756, their fourth and last child, Martha Parke Custis, arrived. Little Martha was fondly called Patsy, a nickname her mother also had.

The Custis household must have been an active place with three children under the age of five. But in 1757, tragedy struck the family again. Despite all the protections her ever-watchful mother could offer, 4-year-old Frances died. Martha's troubles did

White House, where Martha Dandridge Custis lived near Williamsburg, Virginia, was not the same as the White House in Washington, D.C., where the president lives today. John Adams, the second president of the United States, was the first president to live in the White House in 1800. Although the residence is popularly known as the White House, its official name was the President's House. In 1901, President Theodore Roosevelt changed the official name to the Executive Mansion.

not end there, either. Her husband, Daniel, became very ill that year. A doctor was called, but he could not figure out what was wrong. In July 1757, Martha's husband died, leaving her a widow with two very young children. She clung to little Jacky and Patsy and to her faith in God. But she barely had time to grieve. Now she had a vast estate to manage.

Martha quickly became a wise businesswoman, making decisions she had never had to make before. Suppliers in England had to be contacted, and businesses had to be informed that Martha Dandridge

Martha Washington's children John "Jacky" Parke Custis (1754-1781) and Martha "Patsy" Parke Custis (1756-1773)

Custis was now in charge. She refused to fail in her new tasks and lose what Daniel had left her.

At the age of 26, Martha was still a young and pretty woman. She was also one of the richest women in Virginia. It was no surprise that eligible young men started lining up at her door. But Martha concentrated on her business affairs and her children. There was a lot of hard work to do at White House, and Martha absorbed herself in those tasks. Most likely, it helped keep her mind off her sorrows and loneliness. Her friends and family were a comfort to her, and they made sure she got out and socialized. It would have been easy for her just to stay in her house and mourn her losses.

One visit she made to a friend's house was especially important. There, in the spring of 1758, Martha made a new acquaintance, someone who would change her life forever. ᕕ

3 A FATEFUL MEETING

❧❧❧

No one knows for sure how Martha Dandridge Custis met Colonel George Washington. But the family story goes that they met probably in March 1758 at the home of some friends, the Chamberlaynes. Martha and her children had been invited to stay there as overnight guests. Others had been invited for dinner that evening. One of those guests was a tall military man on his way to see a doctor in Williamsburg.

Martha recognized him right away. She may have noticed him before on one of her trips to town. He was easy to pick out of a crowd, because he towered over most men at more than 6 feet (180 cm) tall.

This soldier was making quite a name for himself fighting for the British in the French and Indian War (1754-1763). Tonight, though, he looked thin and

Martha Dandridge Custis meets Colonel George Washington for the first time in 1758.

sickly. The Chamberlaynes invited him to stay the night rather than travel to Williamsburg in the dark when he wasn't feeling well.

Before George left, Martha must have invited him to her plantation home, because it wasn't long before he was planning a visit there. After being treated by a doctor in Williamsburg, George began to feel better. Soon, he sent Martha a letter telling her when to expect him. To Martha's delight, George did come to White House. They got to know each other better, and George met little Jacky and Patsy. After that visit, Martha invited him to come back

George Washington talks with Martha Custis and her children on his first visit.

again, and the next month, he returned.

George Washington frequently came to Williamsburg to meet with the governor of Virginia and talk about the French and Indian War. Sometimes, he came to request more supplies for his soldiers. He was dedicated to his work with the military, but now his trips to Williamsburg gave him a chance to see Martha.

Their visits were interrupted, however, when George was given orders to go to the battlefield to fight against the French once again. George didn't want to lose Martha to one of her many suitors while he was gone. Before he left, he asked her to marry him. They would be married as soon as the fighting ended. Martha accepted his proposal.

While George fought in the war, he and Martha probably sent letters to each other about their daily activities. Martha may have told him about her children and life at White House. George wrote about what was happening on the battlefield. The British army was starting to take the upper hand in the war, and George was optimistic.

In December 1758, he was on his way back to Williamsburg to request more supplies for his troops. The war wasn't over, but he felt he had done his duty. He was ready to resign and planned to do just that when he reached Virginia's capital. On his way, he stopped at his Virginia home called Mount

Mount Vernon is in Fairfax County, Virginia, about 15 miles (24 kilometers) south of Washington, D.C. The house overlooks the Potomac River and has 20 rooms. There are about 15 smaller buildings alongside and behind the mansion. George Washington's father, Augustine, built the main section of the house in the 1730s. He called it the Little Hunting Creek Plantation. George Washington's older half-brother, Lawrence, inherited the property in 1743 and renamed it Mount Vernon. George Washington inherited Mount Vernon in 1761.

Vernon. It was a large estate that included more than 8,000 acres (3,200 hectares) divided into five farms. Each farm had its own workers, livestock, buildings, and equipment. George had arranged for improvements to be made on the house before he left for the battlefield. Now he wanted to check on the progress. He was getting it ready for Martha, his soon-to-be bride.

When he saw that the work wasn't finished, George was disappointed. At first, he thought about postponing his marriage to Martha. But his visit to White House would soon change his mind.

Christmas preparations were well under way when George arrived at Martha's home. Seeing Martha again and feeling the warmth of the Christmas season must have dissolved any thoughts George had about postponing their wedding. He made a hasty trip to Williamsburg, finished his business there, and resigned from the military. Soon he was back at Martha's home for their wedding. On

January 6, 1759, Martha Dandridge Custis and George Washington were married at White House. They were ready to begin their new life together. ❧

Martha Custis' children, Patsy (behind Martha) and Jacky (far right) attended their mother's marriage to George Washington.

4 MOUNT VERNON

ො⚶ා

Martha Washington was happy to turn over the business affairs of her large estate to her new husband. George worked hard to handle the huge plantation. He had to care for hundreds of slaves, make sure the crops were planted and harvested, and see that the horses and cattle were raised properly. He was a good bookkeeper and kept a close eye on the expenses and profits.

On February 22, 1759, the family celebrated George's 27th birthday. They had another reason to celebrate that day, too. George took his oath of office in his newly elected position in Frederick County. He was now a representative in the Virginia House of Burgesses. It was a respected position, since burgesses could make laws for the colony.

But their authority was limited, since England was still in control.

While the House of Burgesses met, the Washingtons lived in Williamsburg. But George wanted to take his new bride to his Mount Vernon home. The thought of moving to northern Virginia was somewhat troubling to Martha. She would have to leave her home, friends, relatives, and the life she had always known.

But in early April 1759, she bravely made the two-day journey with 4-year-old Jacky and 2-year-old Patsy. Their first glimpse of Mount Vernon was a beautiful sight. The house sported a fresh coat of white paint, and trees and flowers bloomed all over the property. The view of the Potomac River was breathtaking.

Martha settled in to the house, placing some of her own furniture, china, and silver here and there to make the place feel like home. Life at Mount Vernon was busy and full for the Washingtons.

When their first spring turned into summer, the muddy roads dried, and visitors started dropping by. They wanted to welcome George's new family to the area. Everyone enjoyed coming to Mount Vernon, and Martha received them graciously. Soon, Martha, Jacky, and Patsy felt right at home.

Martha also had to get acquainted with the slaves at Mount Vernon. She had grown up with slaves at

George and Martha Washington with family at Mount Vernon.

Chestnut Grove and had lived with them at White House, as well. In fact, 11 slaves from White House came along with her to Mount Vernon. Four were skilled craftsmen, while the other seven enslaved people helped Martha with household duties. The Mount Vernon domestic staff now numbered 12. The waiters, maids, a seamstress, and a cook all worked for Martha.

Some slaves worked in the fields caring for the tobacco and corn crops. Others worked as weavers, carpenters, tanners, and millers, who ground wheat grown on the plantation into flour. There were many cattle, sheep, and horses to raise and breed. The fishery, vineyard, and fruit orchards provided a variety of good food for the Washingtons and their staff. In fact, Mount Vernon had everything it needed to function as a self-sufficient community. Even so, the Washingtons often ordered luxury items from England. They enjoyed buying elaborate fabrics, delicious spices, elegant furniture, and special toys for the children.

George Washington oversees the slaves at Mount Vernon during a hay harvest.

Mount Vernon was a comfortable place to live. Each morning at 4:30, one of the housemaids lit the

fire in the Washingtons' bedroom. Another maid would bring in clean water and lay out Martha's clothes. Martha and George ate an early breakfast together. Then George left on horseback to check on his plantation, about a 20-mile (32-km) round trip. While he was gone, Martha spent at least an hour in her bedroom reading her Bible, praying, and thinking. She needed this quiet time before beginning her very busy day.

Her days were filled with caring for the children, checking on the cooking, and watching over the cleaning, washing, and ironing. She supervised the care of the garden, the chickens, and the dairy cattle. She also managed the children's education. A tutor was brought to live at Mount Vernon to teach the children many subjects. Jacky even studied Latin and Greek. Patsy studied spelling, addition, and the Bible.

In the evenings, George often worked on his finances, while Martha sat nearby working on sewing or knitting projects. George shared his ideas with Martha and asked her opinion on matters. Martha was a good listener with a sharp mind and helped her husband make many decisions. She helped him decide what supplies to order and whom to hire. She even may have talked to him about what crops to plant.

One of Martha's finest skills was sewing. She

Martha Washington managed the production of cloth at Mount Vernon to make clothing for more than 300 slaves in the community.

was in charge of the entire textile production on the plantation. The sheep they raised were sheared for their wool, and flax was harvested for linen. Martha taught the servants to spin the wool and flax and showed them how to produce high quality cloth. Then the cloth had to be made into clothes. Most of the clothing was made for the slaves at Mount Vernon and the surrounding community. As an expert seamstress, Martha taught sewing skills to her daughter, her nieces, and some of the young slave girls. The rest of Martha's time at Mount Vernon was spent preparing for the almost constant flow of visitors.

Martha and George rarely disagreed, except about how to raise the children. Martha was over-protective, and George felt she worried too much and spoiled Jacky and Patsy. She didn't like to go anywhere without the children, but George convinced her once to take just Patsy and leave Jacky at home. Martha wrote to her sister Anna Maria about it:

> *I carried my little patt with me and left Jacky at home for a trial to see how well I could stay without him tho we were gon but wone fortnight I was quite impatient to get home. ... I often fancied he was sick or some accident had happened to him, so that I think it is impossible for me to leave him as long as Mr. Washington must stay when he comes down.*

Martha Washington's lack of education was a source of embarrassment for her as an adult. She was particularly bothered by her poor spelling. When she was first lady, her husband would sometimes write a letter for her. Then Martha copied what he wrote so the letters would be in her own handwriting.

Martha worried a lot about her two children, and she had plenty of reasons to be concerned. Two of them already had died, and young Patsy often suffered from seizures. Her doctor didn't know how to help her, and Martha could only keep a watchful eye on her. Martha had suffered many heartaches already, but there would be more to come. There would also be hardships she would endure for her country. Trouble was already brewing in the colonies, and Martha would soon find herself entangled in the turmoil.

Chapter

5 REVOLUTION

❧❦❧

The colonists were angry with England. The French and Indian War ended in 1763 with a British victory. But now, England wanted the American colonies to pay for it. After all, the British said, the war was fought on American soil. The colonists didn't want to pay for the war, so the British Parliament looked for ways to force them to pay. The result was the Stamp Act of 1765.

People in all 13 colonies were forced to buy royal stamps for anything made of paper that could be sold or distributed. Nearly everything needed a stamp—newspapers, marriage licenses, deeds, wills, and even playing cards. The colonists cried out in anger over this new tax that was causing such a burden.

Bostonians protest in the streets against the Stamp Act of 1765.

But they were also angry about the way Britain was governing them. The colonies had no representatives in Parliament. How could England expect them to keep paying more taxes, and why didn't they have a vote when new tax laws were proposed? "No taxation without representation!" became their rallying cry.

Emotions ran high against the Stamp Act. Riots broke out in Boston and New York. The Virginia House of Burgesses called the Stamp Act unfair and illegal. George Washington joined other members of the House to pass resolutions against taxation by Parliament. Representative Patrick Henry spoke out first, saying the House of Burgesses was the only government body that could tax the people of Virginia. As Henry's speech against the Stamp Act grew louder and more heated, the speaker of the House told Henry that treasonous talk would not be allowed.

Henry shouted back, "And if this be treason make the most of it!"

Martha Washington was feeling the effects of the Stamp Act at home in Mount Vernon. The tax was not a great financial burden to her, since she was a wealthy woman. But she knew what it was doing to less fortunate people, especially those living on the newly settled lands of the western frontier. The settlers often had to travel for several days

to reach a place where stamps could be purchased.

Without the stamp, their marriage licenses, wills, and property deeds weren't official. Martha

Patrick Henry speaks out against the Stamp Act in 1765.

and George were both concerned about what the tax was doing to the political rights of the colonists. The issue was less about money and more about representation. What voice did they have in the way they were governed?

Pressure from the colonies led to Britain's repeal of the Stamp Act. But in 1767, Parliament passed the Townshend Acts. These new laws placed taxes on tea, glass, paper, and other products imported into the colonies. Again, the colonists spoke out against Parliament's new laws. This time, their protests led to violence.

Boston was the center of the conflict, and British soldiers arrived there to keep order. But the presence of the British just added fuel to the discontent. On March 5, 1770, the colonists and the British soldiers clashed on the streets. Five colonists died in what came to be known as the Boston Massacre.

Virginians also raised their voices in protest. In the May 1769 session of the House of Burgesses, the burgesses prayed to God that England's King George III would step forward and uphold the rights of the colonists. The actions of the House angered Virginia's governor, who promptly adjourned the meeting.

But instead of going home, the burgesses gathered at a tavern and discussed what they could do.

George Washington was there, and he didn't hesitate to speak up. He declared that the colonists were being treated unfairly. He proposed a boycott of English goods, hoping it would hurt Britain's economy and lead Parliament to repeal the Townshend Acts. The colonists would be asked not to buy any goods shipped from England. The

An engraving of the Boston Massacre by Paul Revere

Cartoon shows the colonists' concern about the tax on tea.

burgesses agreed with Washington and accepted his plan.

Martha Washington would have preferred a

NOTHING WAS THOUGHT OF BUT THIS TAXATION, AND THE EASIEST METHOD OF LIQUIDATION.

T-A-X

'TWAS ENOUGH TO VEX THE SOULS OF THE MEN OF BOSTON TOWN, TO READ THIS UNDER THE SEAL OF THE CROWN.

TAX·ON·
TEA·
3ᵈ per lb

1773

THEY WERE LOYAL SUBJECTS OF GEORGE THE THIRD; SO THEY BELIEVED AND SO THEY AVERRED, BUT THIS BRISTLING, OFFENSIVE PLACARD SET ON THE WALLS, WAS WORSE THAN A BAYONET, different solution to the tax problem. After all, she and most other women liked serving imported tea every afternoon and ordering supplies and luxuries from England. But then Martha read a letter George had written to a neighbor. She especially noticed these words: "[N]o man should scruple or hesitate to use arms in defense of so valuable a blessing." The words "use arms" showed how serious the situation had become.

Martha wanted to do whatever she could to help. She didn't want her husband to go off to war again. Supporting the boycott was important, and Martha probably urged her friends to do so, too. She knew American women could get by without British goods. They could use their many skills to make the things they needed. They could live without the luxuries. Many colonists supported the boycott and learned to live without English goods. Times were difficult, but they were determined to get by.

Mount Vernon continued to function well during the boycott. The Washingtons grew their own food, spun cloth for their clothing, and learned to live without tea. Guests still streamed in, some of them staying several days at a time. Martha always graciously welcomed them to her home.

Several friends and relatives were visiting Mount Vernon on June 19, 1773, when another tragic event in Martha's life took place. Shortly after dinner, beautiful 17-year-old Patsy suffered a seizure and fell to the floor. Martha called for help, while George tearfully prayed for his stepdaughter. Patsy died within minutes, having never regained consciousness.

Martha was heartbroken. George wrote, "This sudden and unexpected blow, I scarce need add has almost reduced my poor wife to the lowest ebb of misery."

Martha "Patsy" Parke Custis (1756-1773)

Jacky, now Martha's last living child, returned home from college to be with his grieving mother.

Martha's grief was deep and lasted for a long time. Even when Jacky got engaged to Eleanor "Nelly" Calvert that year, Martha had a hard time being joyous. The family hoped the addition of Nelly to the family might help fill the void in Martha's heart. On February 3, 1774, Jacky and Nelly were married at the bride's family home in Maryland. George went to his stepson's wedding, but Martha was still too grief-stricken to attend.

During this time, the conflict between Great Britain and its American colonies reached its peak.

In protest against the Townshend Acts, colonists had dumped British tea into Boston Harbor on December 16, 1773. Britain retaliated in the spring of 1774 with several laws. One protest closed down the port at Boston, another required colonists to house and feed British soldiers in their own homes, and still others gave the British more control over the colonies.

The colonists were outraged. Representatives from all the colonies agreed to meet and talk over their grievances. In August 1774, Martha said an encouraging goodbye to her husband as he left to attend the First Continental Congress in Philadelphia, Pennsylvania. Martha was probably anxious as she sent him off; she feared the outcome of the conflict with Britain.

George returned to Mount Vernon later that fall. But within several months, the day arrived that Martha Washington had been dreading. On April 19, 1775, shots were fired in Lexington, Massachusetts, marking the beginning of the American Revolutionary War between Great Britain and the colonies. Martha was sure her husband would be called upon to act, to lead, and to fight.

In May, George left Mount Vernon once again, this time to attend the Second Continental Congress in Philadelphia. In the middle of June, the Congress agreed to officially form an army—the Continental

Army—and appointed George Washington as commander. Martha probably was not surprised when she received George's letter from Philadelphia, dated June 18, 1775:

> *My Dearest: I am now set down to write you on a subject which fills me with inexpressible concern. ... It has been determined in Congress that the whole army raised for the defense of the American cause shall be put under my care, and that it is necessary for me to proceed to Boston immediately to take upon me the command of it. You may believe me, my dear Patsy, when I assure you in the most solemn man-*

George Washington was appointed commander in chief of the Continental Army on June 15, 1775.

*ner that, so far from seeking this appoint-
ment, I have used every endeavor in my
power to avoid it, not only from my unwill-
ingness to part with you and the family,
but from a consciousness of its being a
trust too great for my capacity.*

George was concerned for Martha. He wrote to
several friends and relatives, asking them to look
after her in his absence. He asked people to visit
her and invite her to their homes. If she had too
much time on her hands, he knew she would worry
about him. Martha visited her family in the
Williamsburg area, but she also stayed busy at
Mount Vernon. She managed the household and
oversaw the addition of a new master bedroom and
a study for her husband.

Later that year, Martha could no longer bear to be
separated from her husband. At George's request, she
set out to join him at the Army's winter headquarters
in Cambridge, Massachusetts. She had never traveled
so far from home, but she didn't think twice about
going, because she missed George so much.
Accompanied by Jacky and his wife, Nelly, she set out
on her winter journey, despite the dangers of travel
during the war. All along the way, she was heartened
by the attention she received. People welcomed and
cheered her, and church bells rang as she passed
through their towns. They knew who she was—the

wife of the highly respected general of the Continental Army.

On December 11, 1775, Martha, Jacky, and Nelly arrived at Army headquarters. Visiting her husband and his troops was an eye-opener for Martha. She was surprised by what she saw and heard. She knew George was tangled in the middle of a war, but she didn't realize how fierce the fighting was. She wrote to a friend:

> [S]ome days we have a number of cannon and shells from Boston and Bunkers hill, but it does not seem to surprise anyone but me; I confess I shudder every time I hear the sound of a gun. Charlestown has only a few chimneys standing in it ... they are pulling up all the wharfs for firewood—to me that never see any thing of war, the preparations are very terable indeed, but I endever to keep my fears to myself as well as I can.

But Martha's fears didn't keep her from helping out in the camp. This 44-year-old woman had endured many sorrows already, and she was ready to sacrifice her time and her comforts to help her husband and his soldiers. However, she didn't know then that this war would go on for eight more years.

Other Army officers' wives were also at camp. Two of them—Lucy Knox and Catharine "Kitty"

Greene—would become Martha's friends for the rest of her life. The troops liked having these women around. They were optimistic and cheered up the soldiers, sometimes entertaining them with song and dance. When the soldiers' clothes needed mending, the women got out their needles and thread. When troops were injured, they tore strips of cloth and rolled them into bandages for their wounds.

George liked having Martha by his side. He was a firm, strong general, who never showed fear or discouragement. With Martha, though, George could share his thoughts and feelings. He talked about the problems of holding his small army together and about how difficult it was to get enough clothing and other supplies for his men. Sometimes, though, the problems were so bad that he could not bring himself to talk about them. At those times, Martha knew her very presence was a comfort to him.

Henry Knox (top) and Nathanael Greene were generals in the Continental Army. Their wives often aided the troops.

Somehow, the Continental Army made it through that first winter. By spring of 1776, they had forced the British out of Boston. But then the British went to New York City. The Continental Army—and Martha Washington—could waste no time. They had to get ready to go to New York.

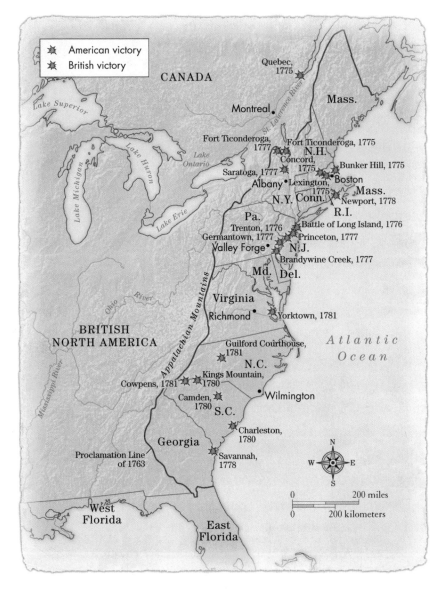

American victory
British victory

CANADA

Lake Superior

Quebec, 1775

Montreal

Mass.

St. Lawrence River

Lake Michigan

Lake Huron

Lake Ontario

Lake Erie

Fort Ticonderoga, 1777

Fort Ticonderoga, 1775

N.H.

Concord, 1775

Bunker Hill, 1775

Saratoga, 1777

Albany • Lexington, 1775 Boston

Mass.

N.Y. Conn.

Newport, 1778

R.I.

Pa.

Trenton, 1776

Battle of Long Island, 1776

Germantown, 1777

Princeton, 1777

Valley Forge •

N.J.

Brandywine Creek, 1777

Ohio River

Md. Del.

Appalachian Mountains

Virginia

Richmond •

Yorktown, 1781

BRITISH
NORTH AMERICA

*Atlantic
Ocean*

Guilford Courthouse, 1781

N.C.

Mississippi River

Kings Mountain, 1780

Cowpens, 1781

Camden, 1780

Wilmington

S.C.

Charleston, 1780

Georgia

Proclamation Line
of 1763

Savannah, 1778

N
W E
S

0 200 miles
0 200 kilometers

West
Florida

East
Florida

*Major battles of
the American
Revolution
were fought
throughout the
colonies.*

But before they left, they were hit by a different
kind of enemy—smallpox. This sometimes-fatal disease spread throughout Boston, afflicting citizens
and soldiers with a severe rash and high fever. The

British started arriving in New York on June 30, and Martha went to Philadelphia to see her husband and to be vaccinated against the disease. She wanted to avoid getting sick so she could stay with her husband. She also hoped her action would encourage the soldiers to get vaccinated as well.

While Martha was in Philadelphia on July 4, 1776, the Continental Congress approved the Declaration of Independence. On July 9, it was read publicly in New York City to a crowd of triumphant soldiers and citizens, who tore down the statue of King George III. This English monarch would no longer rule the colonies, they insisted.

By August, more than 30,000 British soldiers had arrived in New York Harbor. They soon took control of Staten Island and Long Island, and prepared to advance on Brooklyn. Washington's troops were forced to retreat, and the British swarmed the city of New York.

But Washington would not give up. On Christmas Day of 1776, he led his troops across the Delaware River, surprising and defeating the British at Trenton, New Jersey. The Continental Army marched on to Princeton, New Jersey, where the Americans drove the English officers out of their headquarters. Americans began re-enlisting in the Army, and Washington settled in Morristown, New Jersey, for the winter.

Miniature portrait of Martha Washington, painted by Charles Willson Peale and worn in a gold locket by her husband

George and Martha were separated during those winter months. But Martha was not idle at Mount Vernon. She was working hard to increase the production of fabric on the plantation. Congress wasn't providing enough money to keep the American soldiers in uniforms, so she put her servants to work spinning more wool, weaving more cloth, and sewing more clothes.

In March 1777, Martha received word that George was very ill. She left for New Jersey to help him. When she arrived, George was already improving, but the troops were in terrible condition. They were cold, sick, and poorly clothed. Immediately, she started sewing uniforms and knitting socks out of the fabric and yarn she had brought from Mount Vernon. She invited nearby townspeople to the camp to help her. When they arrived, they found a woman they did not expect.

One of the local women said:

I was never so ashamed in my life. … [W]e thought we would visit Lady Washington, and as she was said to be so grand a lady, we thought we must put on our best bibs and bands. So we dressed ourselves in our most elegant ruffles and silks, and were introduced to her ladyship. And don't you think we found her knitting and with a speckled apron on! She received us very graciously, but after the compliments were over, she resumed her knitting.

After their initial embarrassment, the women gained respect for this strong woman who was setting a fine example for them to follow. They realized it was Martha Washington's kindness and compassion that compelled her to work so hard.

One woman wrote about Martha:

There we were without a stitch of work, and sitting in state, but General

Throughout the Revolutionary War, George Washington wore a gold locket around his neck that contained a picture of his wife. The miniature portrait of Martha was painted in 1772 by American artist Charles Willson Peale (1749–1831). Peale believed anyone could learn to draw, and he taught many of his 17 children to paint portraits, landscapes, and still lifes. The most famous of Peale's artist children are Raphaelle Peale (1774–1825) and Rembrandt Peale (1778–1860), named after famous painters. His daughter Sarah Miriam Peale (1800–1885) was probably the first professional woman portrait artist in the United States.

Martha Washington arrives at her husband's Army headquarters at Morristown, New Jersey, in 1777.

Washington's lady with her own hands was knitting stockings. ... She seems very wise in experience, kind-hearted and winning in all her ways. She talked much of the poor soldiers, especially the sick ones. Her heart seems to be full of compassion for them.

Trying not to offend them, Martha made sure these ladies knew that it was very important for American women to be examples of hard work and good business during these hard times.

Martha returned to Mount Vernon that fall. But she was there only a few months before duty again called her to her husband's side at Army headquarters. This time she would travel to Valley Forge, Pennsylvania. She was not prepared for the horrible situation that would meet her there. ❧

6 VALLEY FORGE

❧❦❧

Winter at Valley Forge, Pennsylvania, was miserable for the Continental Army. In December 1777, the tired and poorly equipped soldiers walked through sleet and snow in search of a place to stay for the winter. In wet, ragged uniforms, they set up camp at Valley Forge, about 20 miles (32 km) northwest of Philadelphia. Every night, they tried to warm themselves by the fires so they could sleep. Blankets were scarce, and the ones they had were wet and cold.

General Washington challenged his men to build their own log huts and offered a prize of $12 to the first group who finished a shelter. The men eagerly cut down trees with axes, sawed the lumber, and dragged wood through the snow. Huts soon started

Soldier on duty in the snow at Valley Forge waits for someone to relieve him.

George Washington's Army built crude log huts at Valley Forge during the winter of 1777-1778.

to emerge on the land. Each one was about as big as a medium-sized room and just a little taller than Washington. Spaces between the log walls were filled with clay. Twelve men squeezed into each hut to stay out of the wintry weather.

There was a makeshift fireplace in each hut, but it often didn't work very well. Sometimes smoke filled the room, instead of finding its way out through the opening in the roof, and burned the soldiers' eyes. The men slept on the cold, wet earth. Some of the lucky ones had beds of straw.

Water was scarce. The soldiers had to carry it

from one of the rivers or creeks about a half mile away. To add to their misery, there wasn't much food. On December 23, George Washington wrote to members of Congress, telling them about the awful conditions of the Army:

> *I am now convinced beyond a doubt that unless some great and capital change suddenly takes place, this army must inevitably be reduced to one or other of these three things. Starve, dissolve or disperse, in order to obtain subsistence in the best manner they can.*

As the men starved, so did their horses. More than 1,500 horses died and lay strewn on the ground. Because the ground was frozen, the men couldn't bury the dead animals. Soon, the terrible living conditions led to disease. Many soldiers battled typhus, smallpox, and other illnesses. Nearby communities set up hospitals, but they filled up quickly with troops from other areas. Sick men were forced to stay in their huts in freezing weather. Piles of dirty straw added to their warmth and comfort, but the straw also spread the diseases. Lice carrying the typhus germ lived in the straw. A soldier would die on a bed, and another sick soldier would immediately move onto the straw. It wasn't long before the new occupant became infected. As many as five men might die on the same pile of straw before new straw was brought in to replace it.

Martha was shocked at these conditions when she arrived in February 1778. The men were sick, hungry, cold, and dirty. They wanted to leave the Army and go home. "No bread, no soldier," they chanted. Martha wasted no time. She started working to help them.

George and Martha Washington inspected the poor condition of the troops at Valley Forge.

Again, she had brought fabric and supplies with her from Mount Vernon. Lucy Knox, Kitty Greene, and other soldiers' wives arrived to help. Martha put the women to work making uniforms, gloves, hats, pants, shirts, and socks. The women also went from hut to hut, searching for the soldiers who needed help the most.

They also tended to the emotional needs of the troops. Often, they gathered officers and soldiers into George Washington's headquarters, where everyone was encouraged to sing and even dance. Energetic Kitty Greene worked especially hard to entertain the troops and bring some laughter into their lives. While Martha served coffee and tea, she encouraged her guests to sing and be merry. As usual, Martha brought out the best in her husband at these events. He relaxed and enjoyed the company of his staff and soldiers, sometimes dancing late into the night. It was a time when everyone could forget their troubles, if only for a short while.

Around the camp, Martha listened to the concerns of the soldiers. She showed genuine interest in these brave members of the Continental Army. She tried to make their burdens lighter and encourage them to continue fighting. Spring finally arrived, and with better weather came better health. Food and water were in greater supply, and the men started to have hope once again.

*Martha
Washington
(center) knitted
winter clothing
for the soldiers,
setting an
example for
other women.*

More than 3,000 soldiers died of starvation, exposure, or disease during the terrible winter of 1777-1778 at Valley Forge. Others deserted and went home. The Army may not have held together at all if it hadn't been for George Washington's strength, will, and determination.

Martha also had made a big difference. The troops were strengthened by this gentle angel who took the time to mend their clothes, knit their socks, and sit with them as they died. She had risked so much to be with them and the husband she loved.

Despite all the losses from death and desertion, more than 6,000 soldiers made it through that winter. In May 1778, the Army received great news. France was joining the Americans in their fight for independence. Although many soldiers were still very ill, they were encouraged and determined to defeat the British and end this war. But it would be three more years before the fighting was over. 🐦

Most of the soldiers at Valley Forge lived in log huts during the winter of 1777–1778. Officers rented local farmhouses as their residences and offices. When Martha Washington arrived at Valley Forge, she stayed with her husband in a rented house owned by Isaac Potts. Here, George Washington received local and foreign dignitaries and coordinated the operations of the Continental Army.

7 VICTORY

❧❧❧

Martha Washington spent two more winters at her husband's Army headquarters. In February 1779, she arrived at their new camp in Middle Brook, New Jersey. In November, she joined them at Morristown, New Jersey for another cold snowy winter. She still worried about the condition of the soldiers. Every year, she faithfully set up her sewing circle, but the Army desperately needed money for supplies.

In June 1780, while in Philadelphia, Martha heard about a group of women called the Ladies' Association. They were mounting a campaign to raise money for the Army. Martha joined them without hesitation, even giving $20,000 of her own money to the project. She visited and wrote to women throughout the colonies to encourage them

The Ladies' Association of Philadelphia met together to sew shirts for the Continental Army.

to get involved and to give money. It was a call to action, and the women of America responded. In just a few months, they collected about $300,000, a huge amount of money in those days.

Martha had returned to Mount Vernon, while George continued to fight in the war. Over the next year, the Continental Army had some victories and also suffered some defeats. In September 1781, the Army headed to Yorktown, Virginia, to challenge the British army led by General Charles Cornwallis. On his way, Washington stopped at Mount Vernon. He had not seen his beloved home in more than six years, and his heart filled with emotion as he walked through the doorway.

George Washington "Washy" Parke Custis (1781-1857), grandson of Martha Washington

Martha ran to greet him. Jacky, Nelly, and their four children were there, too. Washington had never met his step-grandchildren before. There before him were 5-year-old Elizabeth (called Betsy and later Eliza) and 4-year-old Martha (nicknamed Patty). Then there was little 2-year-old Eleanor (known as Nelly), and the baby,

5-month-old George Washington Parke Custis (called Washy).

George Washington stayed at Mount Vernon about three days, soaking in the love of his family and neighbors who stopped by to see him. But then it was time for him to go to Yorktown. His step-son Jacky decided to go with him as one of his aides.

The Battle of Yorktown began on October 9, 1781. While Washington and his troops attacked by land, French forces blocked Cornwallis' possible escape by sea. British ships tried to battle the French but were forced to head to New York.

Sarah Franklin Bache (1743–1808), the daughter of Benjamin Franklin, supported the Revolutionary War by helping to raise money for the Continental Army. In 1780, she took over leadership of the Ladies' Association of Philadelphia. Through her efforts, people gave hundreds of thousands of dollars to buy supplies for the Army troops. She also supervised the sewing of 2,200 shirts for the American soldiers.

Trapped between American soldiers and French sailors, Cornwallis and his men had nowhere to go. On October 19, 1781, 10 days after the battle began, Cornwallis surrendered. The American Army celebrated a very important victory of the war.

However, victory was followed by personal sorrow for George and Martha Washington. Jacky was not used to the hard life of an Army camp, and he became very ill with a high fever. He went to the home of his aunt and uncle not far from Yorktown to

John "Jacky" Parke Custis (1754-1781), Martha Washington's son.

get well. But on November 5, two weeks after the British surrender, 27-year-old Jacky died. He left behind his wife and four children under the age of 6. Martha, Nelly, and his oldest daughter Betsy were at his side when he died. They had hurried to be with him when they learned how gravely ill he had become. Martha had now lost all her children.

While the success at Yorktown did not officially end the war, it set the Americans on a course of victory. The British were tired of fighting and spending money on the war. In March 1782, the English Parliament adopted a resolution recommending the war be ended. The Americans signed a preliminary peace treaty with Britain on November 30, 1782, but it would not go into effect until France and Britain agreed on terms of peace. On September 3, 1783, the final peace treaty was signed. The war was over.

On December 23, 1783, at Annapolis, Maryland, George Washington resigned as commander in chief of the Continental Army. He promised Martha he'd be home at Mount Vernon for Christmas dinner, and he didn't let her down.

The family was thrilled to be together at Mount Vernon again. George began getting the plantation back in order. He had been gone for almost nine

George and Martha Washington celebrated Christmas together at Mount Vernon in 1783.

years, and the property needed a lot of work. Martha doted over her four grandchildren and kept the house ready for visitors who might come by at any time. Friends, family, politicians, foreign dignitaries, writers, business people, doctors, and just the curious visited often. Although preparing for guests kept Martha very busy, she wouldn't have it any other way. The steady flow of guests must have seemed endless. In just one year, 423 people visited the Washingtons.

Martha took particular notice of one guest—Dr. David Stuart of Alexandria. Her daughter-in-law Nelly was paying special attention to him. After Jacky's death, Nelly had believed she would never remarry. She was surprised when she fell in love with Stuart. The couple married in 1783, and Nelly's two oldest children, Betsy and Patty, went to live with them. Nelly decided that her two younger children, little Nelly and Washy, could live with their grandparents. Martha and George were happy to raise these two little ones in their home. Once again, Martha had children to fuss over.

Family life filled much of their time, but there was still work to do for the new nation. Mount Vernon sometimes became a meeting place for government officials. In March 1785, George and Martha invited representatives from Maryland and Virginia to meet and discuss how trade would be handled on the Potomac River and Chesapeake Bay. Later, they invited someone from Pennsylvania to join in a trade agreement. This was the first step toward cooperation between the states.

People from other states soon started thinking about how they could work together. In February 1787, Congress approved a meeting in Philadelphia, where all the states could discuss working together as one nation. It was called the Constitutional Convention, and George Washington was there.

Martha stayed at Mount Vernon while her hus-

George Washington speaks to the Constitutional Convention at Philadelphia in 1787.

band helped form a government for the new nation. In a letter to Martha, George told her he had been chosen as president of the convention. But the leaders at the convention had an even bigger job in mind for him. They wanted him to be president of the United States of America. Before there could be an election, though, at least nine of the 13 states had to approve the new Constitution. On June 21, 1788, New Hampshire became the ninth state to ratify the new law of the land.

An election of the convention representatives was held, and the vote for president was unanimous: George Washington became the first president of the country. Although he had enjoyed the past five years of private life at Mount Vernon, his great sense of duty to his country would not allow him to say no. He was willing to serve as the nation's leader. His vice president was John Adams.

Of course, Martha Washington was now the first lady. But she was not happy about George putting them back into public

Gilbert Stuart's 1796 portrait of George Washington hangs in the library at the White House.

service. She knew the presidency would interrupt their family life. Martha wrote to her friend, Mercy Otis Warren:

> *I cannot blame him for having acted according to his ideas of duty in obeying the voice of his country. I am still determined to be cheerful and to be happy, in whatever situation I may be; for I have also learned from experience that the greater part of our happiness or misery depends upon our dispositions, and not upon our circumstances.*

Martha knew she must go with her husband to New York City, the capital of the nation. She had been with him during the Revolutionary War, and she would stay beside him as president. She didn't look forward to being in a public position, but she respected George for being willing to serve his country again. She was duty-bound to her husband, and she also had a deep commitment to the United States. After all, she had helped it become independent. But first, Martha had to put Mount Vernon in order. ✑

8 FIRST LADY

George Washington left Mount Vernon in a carriage and traveled triumphantly to New York as the president of the country. Along the way, church bells rang and cannons boomed to announce his presence. A banner paid for by the women of Trenton, New Jersey, declared, "The Defender of the Mothers Will Be the Protector of the Daughters." Martha Washington wasn't with her husband yet. She didn't attend his inauguration on April 30, 1789, and missed the magnificent inaugural ball that followed several days later.

Three weeks later, after everything was organized at Mount Vernon, Martha packed her things and gathered up Nelly and Washy for the trip to New York. She was welcomed along the way with bells,

Portrait of Martha Washington is on display in the National Portrait Gallery, the Smithsonian Institute, Washington, D.C.

cannons, fireworks, and cheers. People already knew who she was. She was one of their beloved heroines of the Revolutionary War, and now they were eager to honor her as their first lady.

As the first woman to serve in this position, Martha felt a strong duty to represent her country well. She wanted to establish traditions for the new nation and set the standards for other first ladies to come. If the United States was to be considered equal to European countries, events at the capital would have to be spectacular, Martha believed. She would need to plan formal events and dinners that would impress other nations.

Martha's warm personality always shone during these events, making people feel welcome even during the most formal occasions. Abigail Adams, the vice president's wife, helped Martha with the planning. The two became good friends and sat next to each other at formal gatherings.

As soon as Martha arrived in New York, she started hosting weekly receptions called levees. Every Friday, people came to

Abigail Adams was the wife of John Adams, the first vice president of the United States. The first time she met Martha Washington, she was very impressed with her. She wrote to her sister, "She is plain in her dress. ... Her hair is white, her teeth beautiful, her person rather short than otherways. ... Her manners are modest and unassuming, dignified and feminine, not the tincture [trace] of hauteur [arrogance] about her."

their house on Cherry Street for a chance to meet the president and the first lady. The president liked these social gatherings where he could spend time

A guest bows to the Washingtons at a presidential reception in 1789.

with citizens. They were more enjoyable than the rather formal, more serious Tuesday gatherings he held just for men.

Martha welcomed many guests informally, as well. She gladly opened her home to war veterans who traveled to the capital to pay their respects to their general. Knowing what the soldiers had endured for their country, Martha always enjoyed their visits and treated them well. She still had a special place in her heart for these troops who had endured so much for the sake of freedom. It wasn't unusual for her to slip some money to them, if she found out they were struggling financially.

In 1790, Congress moved the capital of the United States to Philadelphia. Because Martha had spent quite a bit of time there during the Revolutionary War, she counted many Philadelphians as friends. The city was more appealing to her than New York. Not only was Philadelphia closer to Mount Vernon, but Martha enjoyed a more active social life there. She went to the theater, enjoyed fancy dances, and attended Christ Church and St. Peter's Church. Martha also loved shopping in Philadelphia, buying dolls, paints, and other gifts for her grandchildren.

Her Friday levees continued in Philadelphia. Wanting to outdo the New Yorkers, Philadelphia society members came to the levees dressed in the finest clothes money could buy. Some of the fancier parties drew criticism from the public and from newspaper journalists, who followed every move the president and his wife made. One stinging article in the *New York Argus* read, "He holds levees like a King, shuts himself up like a King, takes advice from

Philadelphia was the capital of the United States from 1790 to 1800.

his counselors or follows his own opinion like a King." Martha and George were both surprised and hurt by the criticism, but they had too many responsibilities to spend much time worrying about it.

In addition to endless entertaining and tending to the affairs of the nation, Martha also had family matters to handle. She enrolled Nelly and Washy in

The Philadelphia home of the Washingtons

school and started Nelly in dance classes. She made sure 12-year-old Nelly practiced her music, worked on her needlework, and did some drawing every day.

In the spring of 1791, George set out on a four-month journey to tour the Southern states. He heard reports they were not satisfied with his presidency. He wanted to visit them to find out if the reports were true and to win their hearts and their support. Martha stayed in Philadelphia, providing a stable home for her grandchildren and making sure they kept up with their lessons.

George's first four-year term as president would be over soon. Martha looked forward to going home to Mount Vernon. Some members of Congress tried to convince Washington to run again for president. They pleaded with him to keep leading the nation whose Congress had become divided. Federalists believed the federal government should have authority over the states. Anti-Federalists believed a central government was necessary, but states should be able to make their own laws. Leaders were divided, and they needed Washington to unite them. Although Washington tended to be a Federalist, he usually didn't take sides. He was soon persuaded to run again for president.

When Martha first heard her husband was considering a second term, she was not happy. She wanted to go home and escape the public's eye.

However, as always, Martha supported her husband's decision. George was unanimously re-elected as president, and Martha began handling another term with grace and dignity. She had missed George's first inauguration, but she made sure she and her grandchildren attended his second one. The people of Philadelphia celebrated after George took his oath of office, but their joy would be short-lived.

In the summer of 1793, an epidemic of yellow fever hit. Infected mosquitoes spread the deadly viral disease to people throughout the city. It caused damage to the liver and turned the skin a yellow tint. Sometimes, as many as 50 people died in one day.

Martha was worried that Nelly and Washy would get sick, but she hesitated to leave the city without George. The family stayed in Philadelphia until September, when they went to Mount Vernon. In late October, they returned to Pennsylvania, but stayed in the city of Germantown for a few weeks. When they felt it was safe, they returned to Philadelphia. The Washington's avoided the disease, and when the cold of winter arrived, yellow fever disappeared from the city altogether. But about 5,000 people lost their lives that summer.

In the years that followed, there were some joyous occasions for the Washington's. Their granddaughters Patty and Betsy both got married. In January 1796, Martha became a great-grandmother

Map shows boundaries of 1800.

CANADA

Lake Huron

Lake Ontario

Lake Erie

Lake Champlain

Maine

Vt.

N.H.

Hudson R.

Cambridge
Mass.

Conn.

R.I.

New
York

Northwest
Territory

Pennsylvania

Morristown

New York City

Valley Forge

Philadelphia

New
Jersey

Md.

Del.

Mount Vernon

Atlantic
Ocean

Virginia

Kentucky

New Kent
County

N
W E
S

Tennessee

North
Carolina

0   100 miles

0   100 kilometers

for the first time. Patty named her baby girl Martha. A year later, Betsy gave birth to a daughter, Eliza.

As George Washington's second term drew to a close, he resisted the pleas from members of Congress to run for a third term. At that time, there was no limit to the number of terms a president could serve, but Washington did not want to become like a king who reigned for many years. So George

Martha Washington lived most of her life in Virginia. She lived in New York City and Philadelphia while she was first lady of the United States.

and Martha prepared to leave Philadelphia.

There were many exciting activities during the final days of the presidency. They went to parties, attended the theater, and enjoyed concerts. Martha's final Christmas gatherings as first lady in 1796 were crowded affairs. Two months later, on February 22, 1797, there was a huge celebration for George's 65th birthday, which brought him to happy tears. About 12,000 people packed into Rickett's Amphitheater for a ball and buffet dinner. So many people attended,

A huge celebration was planned for George Washington's 65th birthday on February 22, 1797.

one partygoer said, "There was danger of being squeezed to death."

Citizens of Philadelphia said goodbye to George and Martha in many different ways. They fired cannons, flew flags proudly, closed their schools, and held dances. They wanted to make it clear how much the president and first lady meant to them. On their last night in the city, George and Martha entertained a large group for dinner. The newly elected second president of the United States, John Adams, was there with his vice president, Thomas Jefferson. Many tried to hold back their tears and keep the evening joyful, but it was obvious that George and Martha would be missed.

"Ladies and gentlemen, this is the last time I shall drink your health as a public man," George said, offering a toast to his guests at the end of dinner. "I do it with sincerity, and wishing you all the possible happiness!"

The next day, March 4, 1797, John Adams took his oath of office. That night, there was a splendid dinner in honor of George Washington. Now Martha was ready to go back to Mount Vernon. Although she had caught a cold, she insisted on making the journey. Several days later, on March 9, 1797, the Washington's left Philadelphia and headed for home.

9 HOME AGAIN

❧❦❧

Their home at Mount Vernon was a welcome sight when George and Martha Washington arrived on March 15, 1797. "The General and I feel like children just released from school or from a hard taskmaster," Martha wrote to a friend. Although they were now private citizens, their lives were still open to the public. Mount Vernon buzzed with visitors. Hundreds of people, from former soldiers to overseas dignitaries, visited the Washington's.

On rare occasions, when there were no guests, George and Martha spent some time together alone. George wrote in his diary:

> *Unless some one pops in, unexpectedly,*
> *Mrs. Washington and myself will do what*

Mount Vernon, the home of George and Martha Washington in northern Virginia

I believe has not been [done] within the last twenty years by us, that is to set down to dinner by ourselves.

Grandchildren and great-grandchildren lived at Mount Vernon, and the family continued to grow. In December 1797, Martha's third great-grandchild was born—another little girl born to Patty. There was more joy and celebration when Martha's youngest granddaughter, Nelly married George Washington's nephew, Lawrence Lewis. The wedding ceremony was held at Mount Vernon on February 22, 1799—George Washington's 67th birthday. In November, Patty and Nelly both had babies, bringing the number of Martha's great-grandchildren to five. She would eventually have 18.

The great joy and good times at Mount Vernon, however, were soon to be interrupted. December 12, 1799, started like most other days at the plantation. After breakfast, George rode out on horseback to check on the plantation. Shortly after he left, the weather took a turn for the worse. George finished his rounds, but was wet and cold by the time he returned home.

The next morning, George complained to Martha about a sore throat, which continued to get worse. On December 14, Martha was concerned about him and sent for their doctor. When several doctors arrived, they tried a variety of remedies, but nothing

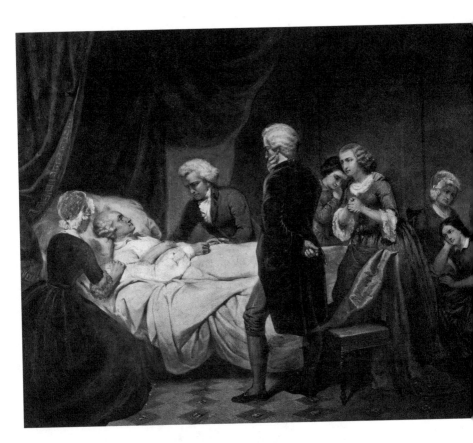

helped. With Martha by his side, 67-year-old George Washington died that day. Martha said, "All is now over, I shall soon follow him. I have no more trials to pass through."

Martha Washington, several friends, and some slaves were the only people in the room when George Washington died on December 14, 1799.

At his funeral on December 18, many people honored George Washington as a great general, a respected president, and an honorable man. Troops came on horseback and on foot to pay tribute to him and to Martha. However, there was one very important person absent from the funeral—Martha

Washington. She was too grief-stricken to attend. George Washington was buried at Mount Vernon, as he had requested.

Inside the house, Martha closed off the bedroom she and her husband once shared and never entered it again. She never again went into George's study. She moved her things to a smaller bedroom on the third floor of the mansion, where she now slept, sewed, and often prayed.

Martha remained surrounded by many members of her family and others who loved her. She continued to entertain guests and kept busy with sewing and knitting projects. She also spent time getting to know her little great-grandchildren better.

George and Martha Washington's bedroom at Mount Vernon, Virginia, as it looks today.

Sometime during the next two years, Martha went to her third-floor bedroom and opened a small chest at the foot of her bed. Inside were letters from her husband that she had saved during their 40 years together. It was a rare bit of time when her family wasn't near, and Martha took advantage of it. She burned all the letters in the fireplace. Perhaps she wanted to keep part of their lives private, secretly binding them together forever. The letters were theirs, not something she wanted to share with the world.

The next two and a half years without George by her side were difficult for Martha. But she continued to enjoy her family and take care of the staff at Mount Vernon. A year after George's death, Martha signed a deed of manumission, a document that officially granted freedom to the Mount Vernon slaves that had belonged to her husband. They became free people on January 1, 1801.

The Washingtons were born into a society where slavery was a fact of life. George Washington became a slave owner at the age of 11, when his father died and left him 10 slaves. Later, he purchased at least 48 more slaves. When Martha Washington's first husband died, she inherited 84 slaves. Over the years, George Washington changed the way he felt about slavery. About five months before he died, he wrote in his will that he wanted all his slaves to be officially set free when Martha died. At his death in 1799, there were 318 slaves at Mount Vernon; 123 of them belonged to George and would be given their freedom.

In 1802, Martha changed her will, leaving the one slave she owned to her grandson, Washy. According to Virginia law, ownership of the rest of the slaves, who had belonged to Martha's first husband, Daniel Parke Custis, would have to be divided equally among her four grandchildren.

One morning in May 1802, Martha didn't come down for breakfast, which was very unusual. She was not feeling well because of a fever that had confined her to bed. For the next 17 days, her family surrounded her and cared for her. Doctors came, and her minister visited.

Even while she was ill, Martha was still making plans. This time, however, she was planning for her funeral and the future of her loved ones. She gave advice to her grandchildren and great-grandchildren, telling them how her religious faith had helped her through all her struggles.

On May 22, 1802, surrounded by relatives, friends, and slaves, 70-year-old Martha Washington died. News spread quickly throughout the nation. The people who had loved her so dearly now mourned her death. Newspapers hailed her as "the worthy partner of the worthiest of men."

This worthy woman would always be remembered, not only for who she was, but for what she did. She gave up time with her husband so he could lead the Continental Army. She left her wealthy

Martha Washington is buried next to her husband in a tomb at Mount Vernon, Virginia.

lifestyle at Mount Vernon to live among the starving soldiers. For the sake of freedom, she used her sewing skills to clothe the troops and encourage them on to victory. Finally, she sacrificed her private life to become a gracious first lady to the people of the United States, setting an example for many more who would follow. ॐ

WASHINGTON'S LIFE

1731

Born on June 2 in
New Kent County,
Virginia, near
Williamsburg

1750

Marries Daniel
Parke Custis on
May 15

1751

Son Danie
Parke Cus
is born

1750

1749

German writer
Johann Wolfgang
Goethe is born

1726

Jonathan Swift
publishes
Gulliver's Travels

WORLD EVENTS

1753

Daughter
Frances Parke
Custis is born

1754

Son Daniel dies
at age 3; son
John "Jacky"
Parke Custis
is born

1756

Daughter Martha
"Patsy" Parke
Custis is born

1755

1756-63

The Seven
Years' War is
fought; Britain
defeats France

Life and Times

WASHINGTON'S LIFE

1759

Marries George
Washington;
moves to
Mount Vernon

1757

Daughter
Frances dies at
age 4; husband
Daniel dies

1773

Daughter
Patsy, age 17
dies

1765

1770

Clergyman and
chemist Joseph
Priestly gives
rubber its name
when he
discovers it rubs
out pencil marks

1759

The British
Museum opens
in London

WORLD EVENTS

1778

Arrives in February at Army head-quarters at Valley Forge, Pennsylvania

1777

Arrives at Army headquarters in Morristown, New Jersey, to care for husband

1775

Joins George at Army headquarters in Cambridge, Massachusetts

1775

1775

English novelist Jane Austen born

1776

Scottish economist Adam Smith publishes *The Wealth of Nations*, heralding the beginning of modern economics

1778

British Explorer Captain James Cook explores the Hawaiian Islands

WASHINGTON'S LIFE

1790

Moves to nation's new capital in Philadelphia, Pennsylvania

1779

Spends winter at Army headquarters at Middle Brook, New Jersey; goes again to headquarters at Morristown, New Jersey in November

1789

Becomes first lady of the United States; moves to nation's capital in New York City

1785

1779

Jan Ingenhousz of the Netherlands discovers that plants release oxygen when exposed to sunlight

1789

The French Revolution begins with the storming of the Bastille prison in Paris

WORLD EVENTS

1799
Husband George
Washington dies
December 14
at Mount Vernon

1802
Dies May 22;
buried next to
her husband,
George, at
Mount Vernon

1797
Husband George
Washington ends
second term as
president; returns
to private life

1800

1795
J. F. Blumenbach
writes his book *The
Human Species* thus
laying the foundation
of anthropology

1799
The Rosetta Stone,
which was the key to
understanding Egyptian
hieroglyphics, is found
near Rosetta, Egypt

1801
Ultraviolet radiation
is discovered

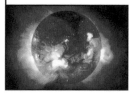

DATE OF BIRTH: June 2, 1731

BIRTHPLACE: Chestnut Grove Plantation, Kent County, Virginia

FATHER: John Dandridge (1700-1756)

MOTHER: Frances Jones Dandridge (1710-1785)

EDUCATION: No formal education

FIRST SPOUSE: Daniel Parke Custis (1711-1757)

DATE OF MARRIAGE: May 15, 1750

CHILDREN: Daniel Parke Custis (1751-1754)
Frances Parke Custis (1753-1757)
John "Jacky" Parke Custis (1754-1781)
Martha "Patsy" Parke Custis (1756-1773)

SECOND SPOUSE: George Washington (1732-1799)

DATE OF MARRIAGE: January 6, 1759

DATE OF DEATH: May 22, 1802

PLACE OF BURIAL: Mount Vernon, Virginia

IN THE LIBRARY

Anderson, Laurie Halse. *Fever 1793*. New York: Simon and Schuster Books for Young Readers, 2000.

Gregory, Kristiana. *The Winter of Red Snow: The Revolutionary War Diary of Abigail Jane Stewart, Valley Forge, Pennsylvania, 1777*. New York: Scholastic, 1996.

Murray, Stuart. *American Revolution*. New York: DK Publishing, 2002.

Simon, Charnan. *Martha Dandridge Custis Washington, 1731-1802*. New York: Children's Press, 2000.

Wagoner, Jean Brown. *Martha Washington: America's First Lady*. New York: Aladdin Books, 1986.

Wilson, Dorothy Clarke. *Lady Washington*. Garden City, N.Y.: Doubleday, 1984.

LOOK FOR MORE SIGNATURE LIVES
BOOKS ABOUT THIS ERA:

Abigail Adams: *Courageous Patriot and First Lady*

Alexander Hamilton: *Founding Father and Statesman*

Benedict Arnold: *From Patriot to Traitor*

Benjamin Franklin: *Scientist and Statesman*

Ethan Allen: *Green Mountain Rebel*

John Hancock: *Signer for Independence*

John Paul Jones: *Father of the American Navy*

Mercy Otis Warren: *Author and Historian*

Phillis Wheatley: *Slave and Poet*

Samuel Adams: *Patriot and Statesman*

Thomas Paine: *Great Writer of the Revolution*

Additional Resources

On the Web

For more information on this topic,
use FactHound.

1. Go to *www.facthound.com*
2. Type in this book ID: 0756509831
3. Click on the *Fetch It* button.

FactHound will find the best
Web sites for you.

Historic Sites

Mount Vernon
3200 George Washington Memorial
Parkway
Mount Vernon, VA 22121
703/780-2000
To visit the home of George and Martha
Washington and learn more about their
lives

Valley Forge National Historic Park
Route 23 and North Gulph Road
Valley Forge, PA 19482
610/783-1077
To see weapons and other equipment used
at Valley Forge during the Revolutionary
War and learn more about what it was like
to live through the winter there

boycott
a refusal to do business with someone as a form of protest

burgess
representative of the Virginia House of Burgesses

deed
a signed document containing a legal transfer of property

deed of manumission
an official document granting freedom to a slave

domestic
relating to the household or family

entourage
people who travel with a high-ranking person

estate
the property and possessions left by a person at death

fishery
a place for raising and catching fish

grievances
formal expressions of a complaint

herbs
plants with qualities that can treat illness

homespun
spun or woven by hand at home

House of Burgesses
part of Virginia's colonial government that created laws

imports
goods brought in from another country

levee
reception held by a well-known person

Parliament
part of the British government that makes laws

repeal
to officially cancel something, such as a law or
a tax

seizure
sudden attack often associated with epilepsy that
sometimes causes a person to shake violently

smallpox
disease caused by a virus and marked by high
fever and skin eruptions

suitor
a man who is trying to persuade a woman to
marry him

typhus
disease carried by lice that causes a high fever,
confusion, and a dark red rash

yellow fever
an infectious, often fatal disease of warm
climates, usually transmitted by mosquitoes

Chapter 1

Page 13, line 5: Cokie Roberts. *Founding Mothers: The Women Who Raised Our Nation.* New York: William Morrow, 2004, p. 235.

Page 15, line 3: Richard Norton Smith. *Patriarch: George Washington and the New American Nation.* Boston: Houghton Mifflin Company, 1993, p. 195.

Chapter 4

Page 37, line 4: Charles W. Stetson. *Washington and His Neighbors.* Richmond, Va.: Garrett and Massie, Incorporated, 1956, p. 72.

Chapter 5

Page 40, line 20: Elswyth Thane. *Washington's Lady.* New York: Dodd, Mead & Company, 1960, p. 34.

Page 45, line 6: Ibid., p. 42.

Page 46, line 12: Stephanie Sammartino McPherson. *Martha Washington: First Lady.* Springfield, N.J.: Enslow Publishers, Inc., 1998, p. 50.

Page 48, line 5: North Callahan. *George Washington: Soldier and Man.* New York: William Morrow & Company, Inc., 1972, pp. 25-26.

Page 50, line 10: *Martha Washington: First Lady.* p. 60.

Page 55, line 1: *Washington's Lady.* p. 131.

Page 55, line 27: Ibid.

Chapter 6

Page 61, line 6: *George Washington: Soldier and Man.* p. 123.

Page 62, line 6: *Founding Mothers.* p. 94.

Chapter 7

Page 75, line 4: Margaret Brown Klapthor. *The First Ladies.* Washington, D.C.: The White House Historical Association, 1981, p. 8.

Chapter 8

Page 77, line 6: *Founding Mothers.* p. 227.

Page 78, (sidebar): Ibid., p. 233.

Page 81, line 4: James MacGregor Burns and Susan Dunn. *George Washington.* New York: Henry Holt and Company, 2004, p. 55.

Page 87, line 1: Carl Sferrazza Anthony. *America's First Families.* New York: Simon & Schuster, 2000, p. 181.

Page 87, line 15: *Patriarch: George Washington and the New American Nation.* p. 294.

Chapter 9

Page 89, line 3: *Martha Washington: First Lady.* p. 101.

Page 89, line 13: Dorothy Twohig and W. W. Abbot, eds. *The Papers of George Washington, Retirement Series.* Charlottesville, Va.: University Press of Virginia, 1998-1999, Vol. 1, p. 281.

Page 91, line 2: *Washington and His Neighbors.* p. 298.

Anthony, Carl Sferrazza. *America's First Families*. New York: Simon & Schuster, 2000.

Bourne, Miriam Anne. *First Family: George Washington and His Intimate Relations*. New York: W.W. Norton & Company, 1982.

Burns, James MacGregor, and Susan Dunn. *George Washington*. New York: Henry Holt and Company, 2004.

Callahan, North. *George Washington: Soldier and Man*. New York: William Morrow & Company, Inc., 1972.

Cunliffe, Marcus. *George Washington: Man and Monument*. Boston: Little, Brown and Company, 1958.

Johnson, Gerald W. *Mount Vernon: The Story of a Shrine*. New York: Random House, 1953.

Klapthor, Margaret Brown. *The First Ladies*. Washington, D.C.: The White House Historical Association, 1981.

"Martha Dandridge Custis Washington." *Colonial Williamsburg*. http://www.history.org/Almanack/people/bios/biomwash.cfm.

"Martha Dandridge Custis Washington." *The White House*. http://www.whitehouse.gov/history/firstladies/mw1.html.

Mount Vernon: Home of America's First Hero. www.mountvernon.org.

Roberts, Cokie. *Founding Mothers: The Women Who Raised Our Nation*. New York: William Morrow, 2004.

Smith, Richard Norton. *Patriarch: George Washington and the New American Nation*. Boston: Houghton Mifflin Company, 1993.

Stetson, Charles W. *Washington and His Neighbors*. Richmond, Va.: Garrett and Massie, Incorporated, 1956.

Thane, Elswyth. *Potomac Squire*. New York: Duell, Sloan and Pearce, 1963.

Thane, Elswyth. *Washington's Lady*. New York: Dodd, Mead & Company, 1960.

Twohig, Dorothy, and W. W. Abbot, eds. *The Papers of George Washington, Retirement Series*. Charlottesville, Va.: University Press of Virginia, 1998-1999.

Brenda Haugen started in the newspaper business and had a career as an award-winning journalist before finding her niche as an author. Since then, she has written and edited many books, most of them for children. A graduate of the University of North Dakota in Grand Forks, Brenda lives in North Dakota with her family.